GO E GOBBLE GONE

Written by **Andrea Butler**
Illustrated by **Brian Karas**

ScottForesman
A Division of HarperCollins*Publishers*

Bradley was given some apples.
Gobble, gobble, gone.

Justine said, "It's not fair.
Bradley didn't share."

3

Bradley was given some oranges.
Gobble, gobble, gone.

Justine said, "It's not fair.
Bradley didn't share."

Bradley was given some watermelon.
Gobble, gobble, gone.

Justine said, **"It's not fair.
Bradley didn't share."**

Bradley got a tummy ache.

Justine said, "Now, that's fair!"